Your Past Does Not Define You

By
Lacreisha Jackson

Copyright ©2021 by Lacreisha Jackson

All Rights Reserved.

No parts of this book may be copied, printed, or distributed without the written permission of the Author and Self-Publisher: Lacreisha Jackson

ISBN: 978-0-578-89470-6

Printed in the United States of America

Table of Contents

Introduction 1

Chapter 1: Early Childhood.. 2

Chapter 2: The Transition A Grandmother's Backbone .20

Chapter.3: "The Bible Belt" Welcome to Oklahoma......26

Chapter 4: The Struggle 34

Chapter 5: Goodbye to Making a Change........................41

Chapter 6: Oral Roberts University Experience 46

Chapter 7: Transition to Texas...51

Chapter 8: Returning Home 57

Chapter 9: Finish What I Started......................................61

Chapter 10: The Big Day Graduation 65

Chapter 11: Minor Obstacles to Texas.............................68

Chapter 12: The Heart of a Grandmother 75

Introduction

I am a young woman who has been through some things that I hope will inspire others. The Bible says we overcome by the blood of the lamb and the words of our testimony. So, I come to you, not with a perfect testimony, but as a person who is trying to reach towards the mark of purpose daily. My testimony is not for your ears to grieve, but to empower someone to let them know they are not the only ones going through, and that they can overcome as well. As I go through my testimony, you will get to know me and some of the struggles I have dealt with and how I have overcome and still striving in these areas. It is a transparent story of faith, redemption, restoration, and a fighter from the past to the present. Not one who is perfect and self-righteous, but someone with flaws, and I continue to strive to be a better person daily. I may have some scars. But I am about to show you how my battle wounds prepared me for my purpose and the woman I have become today. I hope my testimony will teach you how to fight and show you that God gives his most challenging battles to his strongest soldiers. That God will send the Holy Spirit and others to walk with you and guide you throughout your life.

I hope you know you are not alone and that you do not have to be silent about what you have gone through. I am not quiet about what God has brought me through and about His continued restoration in areas of my life. So, I present my testimony to you.

Chapter 1
Early Childhood

As a kid my life was not easy. But I knew from a young age there was a purpose for me. There was a world beyond the struggles I faced. As a kid, I was young and ambitious. As I faced obstacles, I believed in myself and did not believe what my environment had to offer. I stayed encouraged and kept my head held high.

I grew up in Pearl, Mississippi with my mom, Stephen, brother, Trey, and sister, Stacey. My mother was a hard-working single parent who worked in the music industry. She worked an eight to five job, trying to keep food on the table and bills paid. My mother made sure we had everything we needed. Some days food was low, and the lights were cut off, but she made sure we were safe and loved. Her goal was to make sure we got a good, quality education and become all that we could be.

Even though my mom wanted me to get a good education it was not easy. When I was six years old, it was extremely difficult for me in school. I had a speech problem which caused me to stutter. I would often be too embarrassed to read throughout elementary and middle school. Often shying away into the background unless I was called upon. This created a lot of insecurities at a young age and made it extremely difficult for me socially. I believe because of my speech issues it created a lot of problems in my behavior as well. It was hard for me to express myself. I had to go to speech therapy at school and classes away from my peers so I could get my work done. As I got older in elementary school it was extremely hard and embarrassing for me to have this issue. I struggled with my speech for years but later grew out of it.

But just because I had a speech problem, I did not let that limit me. I began to draw a lot at a young age. I used art to express my feelings and what I wanted to say. I often won drawing contests in middle and in Jr. High school. I was known as the girl who could draw in school, and I loved that. I was highly creative at a young age and could draw cartoon characters, shoes, clothing, and nature things. Those were the things that interested me. This one little talent and the gift God gave me helped me get through that difficult time as a child.

I was in elementary school and as a young kid, I was very gifted, but I started to get into a lot of trouble. I had an awful temper. I often got into fights and was suspended from school. I remember in elementary school I required a lot of attention because I missed my mom a lot. She was away from home a lot because of her work schedule. Another reason for getting in trouble was because an older student was bullying me. I was often picked on because of my speech problem and the way I dressed. I was a Pentecostal, so the only thing I could wear to school were skirts, and many students at a young age did not understand that. But once I fought that student, I never was bullied again. From then on, I began to have an overprotective mindset and not let anyone run over me.

My anger issues were so out of control. I got put out of class almost every week. I probably got into fights at least once a month. What really redirected me was one incident where a student was rushed to the hospital because I jumped on him and the kid had an asthma attack and could not breathe. I often ran into altercations but this one was different. I realized I had become the person who had once bullied me. After this incident my teachers chewed me out. As one teacher was yelling at me, in my face, another teacher, who was my favorite teacher, stepped in and took my side even though I was in the wrong. She took me to another classroom and talked to me and I began to cry. This lady held me, and she said, "Lacreisha, I understand you." I broke down in tears and told her I was sorry for everything I had done and was going to try and do better.

As a child I had to find a way to channel my anger issues. So, I turned to music and poetry. When I was in middle school, I started to write music and poetry. As I got older, I would sing and write in my spare time. I picked up this skill to take away anger and take away painful thoughts and feelings. It also became a way to not focus on what was going on in my environment. I figured I could write away a lot of pain.

During this time, I was in middle school and my mother worked a lot. Me and my brother, Trey, and sister, Stacey, often stayed home. I was the youngest, so they would watch me until mom got home. About this time Trey had found a new friend in the neighborhood. My mother allowed him to be the babysitter. He was around 18 years old. He was friendly, and he came off to be a good role model to Trey. We often went to play with him, and his sister and their mom were very friendly. He was always fun to be around. One day he asked me to playhouse with him and he began to touch me inappropriately. I was in the first or second grade and did not understand a lot about sex. He would make me do things I did not want to do, and he taught me a lot about sex. I was very scared, so I did not tell anyone. That brought a lot of condemnation, guilt, and shame. This went on for a couple of years and finally he moved away. At a young age I made a commitment to never be touched until I got married. I really understood the true meaning of sex after I got molested. I kept this as a secret and never told anyone. But I began to throw the thoughts in the back of my head and focus on my mother. I figured my mom had enough problems to deal with. I did not deal with these issues until I got older. But at a young age I tried to cope with those negative thoughts. He also molested other kids in the neighborhood and none of us spoke up because we feared him. He also would bring his friend over to do inappropriate acts. This was a neighborhood secret that most of the kids knew about and neither of us said anything. For years this went on. But years later he came back to the neighborhood. He came to my mother's door and asked if I was there. I was not there. I remember him telling me at a young age that he was going to come back for me and take my virginity when I got older. Those were the thoughts that ran through my head when my mother said he had come back, and I knew what he had come for. I began to thank God that I was not at home that day. It showed me that the Lord was covering me. I did not know later in life that this childhood trauma would affect me, but I did what I thought was best and stayed silent.

I want to encourage anyone who is being molested or has been molested in the past. It is not your fault and I did not know that until I got older. Do not be silent because that is what the enemy would want you to do. Remember you are not alone and there are always people, the most important person being God, who will be there for you. If you stay silent many other people will be victims as well. But through people like me you can overcome because you are talking to an overcomer.

Later, my mother would have me and my sister go to my grandmother's house in Louisiana, from Mississippi, for the summer and holidays. One summer I decided I wanted to stay in Mississippi. I got a new babysitter and it was a wife and her husband. They went to the church I was raised in as a little girl. Every young person loved going to their house. But one day I stayed there, things changed, and it was a little different. One day his wife left to go to the grocery store. He told me to come into the kitchen and he began to tell me how he would feel on young girls. I began to get really scared and started to pray hoping that his wife would come home soon. When he finished talking to me, I went to watch TV. He came into the living room and turned the channel to Jerry Springer, which was an inappropriate show for a child. He began to tell me that I was leading him on and that I was coming on to him. He just began to let me know that I was doing something wrong. He said you sat on my lap and that is what grown women do. He was lying because I could not recall sitting on his lap. So, he began to play mind games with me and manipulate the situation. I begin to feel bad as if I had done something wrong. So, he went to the kitchen and I went to the back of the house. He called me into his room. He began to say things like I had done something wrong. He shut the door and another young person that was there began to scream my name because she could not find me. She came into the room and grabbed me and told me to leave the room. I knew she was being protective and was looking out for me. When I left the room, I heard his wife open the front door and I ran to her. So, I went home and told my mom I did not want to go back over there, and she said ok. I knew exactly where this was going. This man and his wife were members at our church, and we went to church every Sunday and kept it to ourselves. At a young age it was difficult to go to church while trying to cope with all these things that were going on. This kind of situation made me act out a lot and I did not know at the time that it was affecting me socially, spiritually, physically, and mentally. That was the last time they babysat me, and I started going back to my grandmother's again like I previously did every summer.

Through this situation I learned that the enemy was trying to destroy my faith at a young age in my belief system in God. Little seeds of doubt were being planted. Me being uncomfortable in church. Nervous to walk to the restroom because he played an instrument and I had to walk past him. While in church I began to start trying to fight mentally in the house of God where I thought was safe. But during that time my prayer life began to get stronger because when I went to church, I began to say small prayers when I got scared or nervous. Little did I know God was developing a strong prayer life.

A strong prayer warrior whom I loved staying with was my grandmother. We began to go to our grandmother's for the summer because my mom needed help. So, she kept us in Louisiana for every summer. My grandma stepped in and this was a start to a pure relationship that gave me spiritual guidance and became a covering. She did her best to make sure her grand kids had everything they needed, and we never went without. We ate three meals a day and maybe a couple of extra ones. Anything I wanted she gave to me and never treated her grandkids differently. She treated us all the same and gave all of us enough attention. A lot of things that I went through previously. I did not tell her because I felt guilt, shame, and as if a lot was my fault, so I kept a lot of things to myself and stayed silent.

My grandma provided a safe environment but with about 8 grand kids and babysitting everybody's kid in town, some things would slip through the cracks. I thought that this was a safe place and I did not worry about being molested anymore.

So, in the summers we had to be there with our cousins. The very thing that I was running from meets me at my grandma's. At the time I was in middle school and my cousin would get drunk and come into my room and just feel on me. I felt horrible, so I would sit there numb in fear. Praying that this would stop. At times I felt as if God was not there. So, this went on for many years. Until I later transitioned out of my grandmother's home. For him not to touch me I started to sleep with my grandma because he was too scared to come in there. I would even try to sleep with my sister and have her to hold me at night, so he would not be able to touch me. She never knew why I would cuddle in her arms so close like a baby, but that was the reason why. She was like a guardian angel and sometimes I thought of her as being my mom because she stood in so many areas of my life. Throughout those years I was exposed to a lot and because of the molestation my body began to go through a lot of changes that I did not understand. I began to become very sexually curious. At a young age I was exposed to pornography through another relative's house that I was left at. I remember having this dirty feeling after I watched it and always would take baths after watching it thinking it would make me clean the dirt off me and it made me feel better.

But many people would be upset for years for being exposed to sexual activity. I had many doors that were opened and struggles that came when I was younger and that affected me, as I got older. But later on in life, I learned this word called forgiveness. Now forgiveness did not happen overnight. Once I got older, I learned how to set boundaries. The pain, guilt, and shame I no longer carry.

But today I have forgiven him. I may not understand why I went through all that. But I will always remember my sister would tell me that sometimes God gives his toughest battles to his strongest soldiers.

Prayer of Forgiveness

Lord I pray for the ones who have done me wrong. I pray that in every area of my mind that I am healed from renewing my mind daily. I forgive not just by my words but by my actions. Making sure I do not act upon or do what was done to me to anyone else. I pray that anyone that has gone through a similar situation will be able to forgive as well. Not holding anger grudges or any hatred in their hearts. I also cast down the spirit of fear that you will sleep through the night with a peaceful mindset. Knowing that god is your covering and that god has not given you a spirit of fear. But a sound mind. So, we seal this prayer knowing that we must forgive 100 times over again and knowing that if god is for us then who can be against us. Amen

Lord Purify Me Prayer

God, we come to you humbly asking you to purify your children from all thoughts that are not like you. Make us whole in areas where we have been damaged. May we not carry the shame and guilt of the past into our future. We come to you as children who are naked with impurities, who need to be clothed with your purity. Make us whole again like we were created to be. We personally forgive and I forgive the ones who have violated us. As your word says forgive them for, they know not what they do. Not discrediting what the people have done. But we know God will bring judgement upon them. Amen.

Young Hustler

As a kid my favorite part of school was lunchtime because I knew I was going to be able to eat a meal. Now my mom provided but we still had to struggle a little. I knew at school all my worries went away. But that never made me feel as if I had enough. I always felt as if I needed more. I knew there was money out there and a world I had not discovered yet.

I remember my brother Trey would get home from school and leave home for a couple of hours and would come back with money and food. While my mom was at work I was never allowed to go outside. But I wondered what my brother Trey was doing to get money. So, I left the house one day to find out that my brother was racking leaves in the trailer park to get money. When I saw him doing that it brought tears to my eyes. He was trying to be the man of the house at a young age. So, I asked him could I join him and how much he was making. He made ten dollars a yard. So, I joined him one day. At a young age we began to earn money. At a young age I knew I could make money and provide for my family. The money that I made I would save so when we got into hard time, we had something to fall back on like little things we could eat on. For a while, my mom did not know because we knew we were not supposed to go outside. But we finally told her after my brother got caught not being home after getting off work. She was proud of us and we put a smile on her face.

We tried to get money and things that we needed at a young age. A relative I knew always would have the latest things and I asked how he was getting it. So, he told me he was stealing it at the store. So, I asked how, and I began to go to stores and steal. One thing that I learned when you are dealing with poverty you will do anything to keep food on the table and make sure you would not go without. But one day something happened that shifted my mindset. I was in the store and wanted a pair of earrings. So, I took them, and the owner saw me. I took off running and ran out the store. God began to speak to me and let me know I was going on the wrong path. So that was the last time I did that. I learned a valuable lesson when I was young. Some things in life you do not need, and God will give you just enough to make it through.

A Daughter's Bond

One thing my mom installed in us at a young age is to believe in God. My mom tried to raise me Trey and Stacey up in church. We were raised Pentecostal, so we went to church almost every day of the week. Also, she made sure we had food. I remember she would ask what we wanted to eat, and she would prepare it for us. When my mom had it, she would prepare it for us. One thing that I admire about my mom is she taught us how to pray. There were sometimes I would walk into the house and hear her crying and praying to God. So, I would get on my knees and pray whether we were going through good or bad times. My favorite moments with my mom were in the morning. She would gather us together in the morning and would pray over our day. My mom worked long hours because she worked for a record label called Malaco Records and song for the Mississippi Mass choir. I loved to go to choir rehearsal with her because I loved music, so I took my homework with me just so I could hear the music. I looked up to my mom and admired her. So as a young child this was the only perception I had of my mom while she was raising us.

A Mother's Prayer

I pray for every mother who is a single mother and doing everything on her own. That she is not forgotten and that every seed that she has invested in her children. Nothing will return to her back void. I pray for every mother's strength that she will be strong in times that are hard. That the mothers will remember God will not put more on them than they can bear. I release a double portion of grace, peace, and strength to withstand anything coming their way. Amen

Hard Times

My mom was single for a while but finally got married. While I was 8 years old my mother got married to my stepfather. He was a funny man and was a great provider. It was exciting to see my mom happy and stable. I remember when she got engaged. I was happy I was going to have a father. As a kid I learned that everyone is always looking for love or to love someone. At that time, I thought that was what we needed.

A couple of months everything was fine until things started to shift in his attitude then the verbal abuse started. We later learned that he had a lot of anger issues and was very abusive. Later in their marriage my stepbrother came along. My brother was 3 months when he came into the situation. I remember my stepfather abusing my little brother and my stepbrother that he later brought into the marriage that he had before he married my mom. He would throw my brother around the house and wipe him with electric cords from the TV. Or anything he could get his hands on. I remember the very first time I saw him whoop my little brother he threw him into the air and let him drop to the floor. I thought Oh Lord please keep my brother and do not let him die. This was a very painful thing to look at. Another incident happened on my brother's birthday when he told him to stop crying and he would not, so he opened his mouth and stuck a knife in it. I thought then that he was going to kill him. He also would whoop me with electric cords just in my underwear.

Many memories about that marriage during that time were very painful. I can remember as a child getting whooped so badly that sometimes it burned to take a bath. The only thing I could think of, as a child was where did my mom find this guy. Now that I am older, I think back and realize that we barely even knew him before they got married. He just showed up. He had a lot of hate in his heart towards my brother Trey and Sister Stacey. I remember him always trying to make my sister mad just to have a reason to whoop her and with Trey he would always try to throw him around. But we could only take so much.

One night he had told my brother Trey that he was going to whoop him when he got home. My brother told us he will hit us no more. Later that night we ran away. That night we slept behind the skating ring next to the dumpster. Many people would think that was a horrible place to sleep. But at the same time, I could remember having this level of peace and being able to sleep without hearing someone yelling or trying to put their hands on me. Later that night, the police had found us with their dog. That night I remember praying to God to take away my stepdad and all the hurt and pain. Later that night we were sent back to our home. But that night an officer came back to our home and got us because she did not think it was safe. I was happy but did not know where we were going. I remember the lady officer smiling and saying she would come back and get me, and she did.

I remember the feeling that I was not forgotten. All my prayers had been answered and God had sent an angel to help us out. I did not know where we might be going. I just knew that help came, and it was a feeling of relief, and it was a feeling that I could not explain. I know that was God covering us and watching over his children.

Foster Care Experience

We went to this house with a lot of kids. We had gone to a foster home. I was in an unfamiliar environment and was very scared. We stayed with an older white couple, which was different for me. I remembered as we arrived, we had to talk to a guy who was our social worker. He just said that we were in a safe place and nothing was going to happen to us. I believed him, but I was worried about my mother. The social worker let me know everything was going to be ok. He also ensured me that I would see my mom again. He was a nice guy and always made me feel better. I always knew I was going to hear from my mom through the social worker or have a visitation. But I was always hoping to go home. The social worker always had something good to say. He made sure we were not being mistreated. Which I really appreciated. It was weeks before I could see my mother. I believe a month had gone by before I could see my mother. There were many nights I stayed up crying wondering when my mother was going to come and get me. It was the very first time I had ever felt lost in life. I remembered the feeling of being abandoned. I thought my mom had given us away and had given up.

There were many lonely nights. A lot of times I felt sad not fully understanding our situation. My first foster home was different for me. We had bump beds and Trey and Stacey were with me as a well, so we were together. We had three meals a day. I remember we had alarms in every room because kids would run away.

This couple was nice and treated my brother and sister well. We lived in a nice home and had a farm with a lot of animals. We ended up staying with this couple for a while until Christmas. I remember them asking us what we wanted for Christmas and I was really shocked because no one had really ever asked us what we wanted for Christmas. We told them we do not celebrate holidays because it is against our religion. I remember her saying all kids want gifts and I got excited. She said write out what you guys want, and I will get it for you, so we said ok. I just wanted some toys. I thought to myself these people really care for us and I never felt so loved and cared for in my life, so I tried my best to be on my best behavior.

A couple of months had gone by and they spilt me up from Trey and Stacey. I remember I would cry all night long because I had never been apart from them. I could not sleep at all. The elderly couple asked did I want to get adopted by them and I told them no and that made me cry even more. Being apart from my siblings forced me to talk to other youth. But I really did not say too much because I was sad. They moved another girl into my room, and I began to get to know her, but that all changed. I thought I knew her very well, but I did not. One night I was laying in my bed and I heard her talking. She began to talk to herself. I remember her saying that she saw angels and they told her to jump off a bridge. The first thing I thought was oh my gosh this girl is crazy, and I wish my sister was there because I was scared. She got up and was on the edge of her bed just talking. Then she got up and began to walk towards my bed. As she approached me, she reached her hands out as if she was aiming for my throat, and something told me to scream, which then I did not know it was God. I began to scream, and the elderly lady ran down the hall and began to ask what was wrong. She immediately knew that the girl was the problem. The couple had decided that they did not think it was healthy for me to be away from my siblings and saw being there was not doing me any good. Finally, they placed me in a second foster home with my brother and sister. I was happy when we reunited.

While in foster care, I started a new school. My first day of school I felt like an outsider but soon I found a friend who was in foster care in my class and his name was Zack. I found him on the playground and started to talk to him. I found out that he had been through a lot. He had also been in the system for years. Hoping that one day his mom would come get him. But I encouraged him and let him know that his mother loved him and was coming back.

As I went to this school, I was quiet and kept to myself. Many days I was sad hoping one day that I would go home. One day I had asked to go to the restroom and another girl asked to go as well. I went to the restroom and this girl tried to bully me. But the teacher came in and broke the fight up. I started to cry and the teacher pulled me to the side and she said that she understood. I had to be put in after school suspension because of the fight. But later the girl approached me and told me that she was sorry. She said she did not know I was in foster care. When attending this school, I tried to keep it to myself that I was in foster care because it was embarrassing.

One day I had come home from school and my foster mom said you have a visitation to see your mom. I remember being so excited and thinking my mom does love me. When I came into the building and went into the room. I saw my mom but with her was my stepdad. I was wondering why he was there and thinking what he could possibly have to say to us. I blamed him for putting us into foster care and did not care too much for him anymore. At this point I really did not understand why my mother was still with him. While we were visiting our mother, another guy walked in. I did not know who he was but remembered him sitting in the lobby. My mom introduced him and told us he was our birth father. This had really shocked me. I had never seen my birth father in my entire life. I remember him looking at me and saying so you are the one I have not seen. I just looked at him. During this time, I could tell that my stepdad was unhappy in his presence. At this point I was wondering how my mother felt in this whole situation and did she miss us. But I did not worry I was just happy to see my mother.

As time went by Christmas and Valentine's day had passed and we changed to two different foster homes. Months have gone by and we did not return home. I felt abandoned and not cared for. There were nights I did not go to sleep. I just stayed up at night crying hoping my mother would come.

Finally, that day had come. I was going home. My social worker had come to get me my sister and brother. As we returned home our mother was still with our stepdad, I remember it being weird that we were in the same house as him. I also remember what I was going to tell my friends about what I was really going through. I figured I was going to tell them that I was off with family for a while and moved back. I thought this was too embarrassing to tell anyone. So, I lived with this as a secret my entire life.

As time went on Darrel my stepdad started to go back to his old angry ways. My brother Trey moved out leaving my sister Stacey and I to defend ourselves. But things got worse and Stacey became our stepdad's new target. After long workdays he would come home angry and taking it out on my sister and me. He often hit us with our clothes off with electric cords. It was very painful for a skinny little girl. But one day I said I was going to talk to him and tell him how I felt. So, as we rode home one day, I told him you really are a good guy it is just hard for you to experience your feelings. His eyes began to water up and he smiled at me as if he was a kid. After that my stepdad never whipped me again. But he continued to hit my stepbrother Paris and sister. I felt guilty a lot of times when they would get whipped because I was not getting one. Even though I was not his target they still had to suffer and that brought sadness to me, so every time something would happen, I would try to make him happy. I knew it was a way to distract him, so he could be nice to them. A lot of times it worked, but sometimes it did not, and it would hurt me a lot because I could not defend them.

After 5 years of marriage my mother threw in the towel and called it quits. I remembered this day as if it was yesterday. I went into their room and my mom and stepdad were sitting on the bed and he said let's talk. He mentioned that he was sorry for all that he had put us through and that he and my mother were getting a divorce. I was so excited with joy at that time. I thought now we could have a peaceful home. But I knew financially things were going to be a little rough. Darrel was the provider and made a lot of things easier for my mom. One thing he did do was providing. At this age I thought love came from things. We had all the latest things all the name brand clothes. I had learned, as I got older that this was a form of conditioned love. I understood him once I met his mother. His mother was abusive to him, which he later told me as he and my mom were in the process of getting a divorce. So, I understood why he was like that toward my brothers and sister. But I did not lose my faith. I turned to God and other outlets.

When they got a divorce, my stepbrother left to stay with his biological mom. I will never forget him. As I got older, I often thought about him and prayed for him hoping that he was ok. I saw him one time after they got a divorce and never heard or saw from him again. I missed him a lot because I would walk him to the bus stop and help him get ready for school. We had some precious memories. But I pray he had a better life where he went and that one day, we can reunite under better circumstances.

Prayer of Peace

I pray for anyone who is going through a difficult time at home and it feels as if you are in a storm. I silence the wind that is coming up against you in your life that represents confusion and dysfunction. I pray that God will remove what is coming up against your household. Also, strength to withstand the trails coming against your family. So, I pray peace, love, and joy that will abide in your home. Amen

Chapter 2

The Transition

A Grandmother's Backbone

A couple of months after the divorce, my sister Stacey mom and I moved to Grambling, Louisiana. I was about 13 years old and this was exciting to me. Also, a fresh start for my family and me. We frequently visited Louisiana on holidays, weekends, and summertime. I was familiar with the environment. We were close to family. We would also be living with my grandmother for a while. While we were transitioning as a family my mother entered another relationship after a couple months of her divorce. One day when I came home, he was sitting in the living room. He was a producer. I did not trust him at the time because I was trying to look out for my mom while in Jackson Mississippi. But while we were in Mississippi, he came around but did not give us any trouble.

So, the big move came were we transitioned to Grambling, Louisiana. It was an exciting time we laughed and talked the whole way driving down there. Louisiana was much different from Mississippi. Mississippi was much more diverse, and Louisiana was an all-black town. I was a little nervous to start school and to go places.

As I transitioned to live with my grandmother things were different. She got me up for school did my laundry and cleaned my room. Grandma did everything and made sure everything was taken care of. We did not have to want for nothing. She was like a guardian angel that looked out for us. She made sure we went to church that made me curious about being Baptist or searching and digging deeper into Christianity. Living with my grandma really made me think about my purpose and what I wanted to do with my life. I believe most of my wisdom came from my grandma at a young age. She would have small talks with me that would motivate me and always talk about God around me. So, at a young age I knew the Bible and read it a lot. I may not know everything about the word, but I read it. At that age I also said I am just trying to be a good person make it into heaven and hopefully God will see that.

A couple of months went by and my mother got engaged to the guy who kept coming over my house in Mississippi. Later he moved in with my grandma as well. I did not like it because I did not want a dad. Finally, I got over it. Him and my mother moved to Shreveport Louisiana where they settled for a while. I really did not want to move again. My mom did not ask so I did not say anything. We stayed with our grandmother. My grandmother began to take on the responsibility as a parent.

Education

But also, with my grandmother my aunt and uncle stepped in to help. They would bring food to the house and come to check upon us. While with my grandmother, I started to slack in my classes and I tried not going to school. So, my aunt stepped in and started making me go to school so I did. I was skipping classes because I was having a hard time not having my mom there. My teacher would ask me personal questions. She thought I was lying but I really was telling the truth. This was my English teacher. At one point she tried to get me to read in front of the class. I said no because at the time I had a stuttering problem and she got mad. So, I told my aunt I felt as if she was picking on me. My aunt came up there and gave her a piece of her mind and I never had a problem with that teacher anymore. She was nice to me afterwards.

While in sixth grade I learned that I had a lot of family that lived in Louisiana and went to school with me. I got to know a lot of upper classmen that put a chip on my shoulder. While living there I found out I had brothers and sisters that went to the high school when I was in seventh grade. They were the popular kids because my family was really known around town.

Self-Image

As a teenager you are just trying to get to know yourself and you barely know who you are. As I went through a lot of transitions, I needed a lot of guidance on figuring out who I was. I moved around a lot and had been in several homes, so I tried to stick with just being a good person and what I was taught at church. Also, I took some morals and values that I had learned along the way.

While I was 14 in 7th grade a girl made up a rumor about me because I was a virgin. I was taught to stay a virgin until marriage and that was part of my religion. I told some girls about me not having sex, but they did not understand because none of them were virgins. One girl in the group went around school telling people that I was gay. My best friend came back to me and told me. I was hurt, ashamed, and embarrassed to walk the halls of my school. I confronted her about it, but she denied it. My mom or dad should have been speaking to me, but I did not have them there. So, I started to struggle with the small voice in my head saying *you're gay*. It would be there in my head and come and go. This started as an issue at a young age that I would have to face later in life.

The first girl who made a pass at me I would have never known she would try anything. She was the popular girl in high school much older than me and I was in Jr high. She could get any guy she wanted. I looked up to her so much because I thought she was cool. One day I stayed the night at her house, and we all slept in the same bed. The girl tried to sleep with me in a sexual way. I felt so uncomfortable. I hurried up and got out the bed, ran to the restroom and did not come out for a while. But I did not let it happen because I was really not into girls and was not sexually active. The next day we acted as if nothing happened, but it was awkward for me. In my mind I started to think there must be something wrong with me. I am being called gay and a girl is trying to sleep with me. So, I reached out for help because my mind was all over the place. So, I told my sister about the rumor and the girl that made a pass at me. She told me I was not gay. She also told me that I needed to pray. That made me feel better.

I pray that anyone who has been bullied and have been called all types of name. That you are who God created you to be. You are a diamond ready to shine bright. I pray for the one who is fighting peer pressure that they will have people that will stand in their corners and fight for them. For you are a gift and no matter who you are, or your sexual orientation God still loves you no matter what.

Religion

When I lived in Mississippi, I had to go to church almost every day of the week. I was raised Pentecostal. As a child religion was difficult to me because a lot of it was forced and not me willingly going to church. A lot of times a lot of my discipline came from the church, which was not always a good thing. Often my pastor would call me out when he was preaching and embarrass me and tell me to stop talking in church. I guess my mom saw him as a father figure to me. I often acted out in church. Getting kicked out of Sunday school or being corrected by the pastor and his wife. I felt that religion was a lot of rules and if there were so many rules I would rather go to hell. I often had a difficult time receiving the message because I was often getting in trouble by people at church, so I often became rebellious and did not really care to be in church at a young age.

As I got older, I started to get closer to God and that was my grandmother's influence. I had gotten baptized and gave my life to God when I was 13 but when but in 8th to 9th grade there were different influences in my life. I had been exposed to drinking and the party life, which it is not a problem with hanging out and having a good time. But I used it to deal with my emotions in an unhealthy way. So, I began to war with God on the inside. I went to church and read my word every night and tried to stop partying. I told God I was going to be a good person. But I still felt like I was missing something in life like purpose. I was always a deep thinker and prayed a lot. Part of the reason I was close to God was because my mom taught me how to pray. Almost every day I would hear my grandmother praying and those prayers of a grandma got me through. Even though at a young age I was slipping up I was still close to God. I knew God as a father, mother, and friend.

Parties

When I hit high school the party life had hit. I was not thinking about college and was not getting good grades. I was thinking about the party life. All my friends partied, and it was the thing to do on the weekends. I started to drink on the weekends as well and did not care. But I still knew that God was pulling on me. I tried not to think about it. All I knew was hanging out and having a good time. But I never got wasted or really drunk. I just got a little tipsy enough to have fun. I always knew my surroundings and how I would get to a place and get home. I was always alert. But something happened to me that changed my whole life and I will never forget that night.

I was really missing my mom and was confused in my head. So, I said I am going to go out to party and drink to clear my head. I did, and it was the first time I really got drunk. I got home and looked at myself in the mirror and burst out crying. I was really a mess and really hurting. So, I got on my knees and started to pray. I asked God to send me good guidance. I told God I was done running and I am giving my life to him. I asked God for a little brother or sister, a new environment, and to be more positive. Little did I know that this prayer would be answered very soon.

God was about to show up. In fact, he was already working in my favor. God quickly came to my rescue and stepped into my situation. Not the way I thought he would have come. But they say be careful what you ask for and it may just happen. That prayer came true for me.

Chapter 3

"The Bible Belt"
Welcome to Oklahoma

I was in my 9th grade year going to school in Louisiana. While I was at school I was called into the office because someone wanted to speak with me. So, I walked into an office and a lady was there. She began to ask me about the condition of my grandma's house. I said we are fine and that my grandma was taking care of us. As she talked, she began to talk to me and tell me she was a social worker. She said someone had called her and that we were living in a bad condition. So, I wondered who called social services on my grandma. She began to tell me that when I got out of high school, she would help me go to college. But in my mind, I am like lady you're trying to take me from my grandma. I don't want any of your help. Now my grandma's house was in bad condition. But we were still happy, and we never went without a meal and we wore nice clothes.

Later that evening I got off the bus at my aunt's house because they told me to go there after school. I walked in the house and saw my and grandma at the table. They looked as if someone had died. They said pack all your clothes you are going to a family member's house. So that is what me, my sister, and brother did. The next day some of our family came from out of town and we had to have a family meeting. So, my uncle Jeff and my aunt Sue began to tell us that we needed to come stay with them and go to school because grandma can no longer take care of us. Her house was in bad condition and it was not safe for us. Also, I believe we probably would have ended up in foster care again if they wouldn't have stepped up. So, as they began to tell us this, my sister and I began to cry. So, they told us go to school the next day take pictures with your friends and we will leave the following day. So, when we got to school, we began to tell our friends. The news traveled so fast through the school you would have thought someone had died because everyone was emotional. As a teenager I was very private, so I did not tell them the reason why we were leaving because I was ashamed and embarrassed.

The next day we were on the road. I remember this like it was yesterday because I cried the whole way to Oklahoma. We were going into an unfamiliar environment and we knew no one there. My aunt Sue and uncle Jeff then took on the responsibility of being our legal guardians basically you could have called them our new parents. During this time, I was 15 years old.

So, when we finally made it to the house. We pulled up to this nice brick house in an upscale neighborhood. We entered our room, and I was smiling because it was nice. My sister and me shared a room. Their daughter also lived with us. She later became the little sister that I had prayed for when I was younger. As time went by, we began to adjust. My sister and me went to different schools so that was difficult for me at first. The school we went to only had like ten black people, and I had to adjust to a new culture because where I came from Grambling Louisiana is a town with majority African Americans. At this school I did not want to be anyone's friend because I knew I was going to move back to Louisiana one day. I did not know that I would never return to Louisiana until later in life. But I began to make a lot of friends and the kids were always asking me to hang with them. So, I began to adjust to my new school because I was accepted. Which was different for me because I came from an all-black town.

Little did I know that the prayer I prayed. God began to answer it. I did not notice it, but it took a while for me to see it come to pass. God stepped in and began to change my situation overnight. It was not easy, and it did not come to me in a beautiful picture. My transition from my home was difficult. But God knew what I needed.

Greenwood Christian Center

As time went on, we began to go to this church called Greenwood Christian center. It was a lively church with a lot of young people. I remember our first service that Stacey and I had gone to. It really shocked me because this was what I prayed for. The people were free with their worship, which I really loved. My uncle Jeff was on the worship team and him and my aunt Sue would be in church plays. They were active in the church, which I really admired. They had a strong Christian foundation. I remember saying this church is different. The atmosphere was like a sweet fragrance of perfume. The youth there were really seeking God and I had never seen that before. They danced in church and were not judged.

One day at church I heard a prophet was coming to the church. I did not know what that was. But I soon found it out. When she taught, she began to speak into people's life. It scared me. A lot of witchcraft was done in Louisiana and I thought that was what she was doing. So, she pulled me out of the crowd and began to tell me certain things I dealt with. I was low key embarrassed. But little did I know God was setting me up for restoration and healing.

Later that week my Aunt Sue and Uncle Jeff asked did we want to go to an encounter. My sister and me asked what that was. So, it was a 3-day weekend at church where young people got together. They would teach sermons all weekend. So, the encounter had come, and it really was powerful. People would tell their testimonies. It made me feel as if I was not alone in some of the things I had gone through. But the most difficult part of the weekend was the small groups. In these small groups you had to open up. We had a small group leader. She was Jamaican and very cool. I loved her accent and her personality. In our small group she began to talk about grace and mercy. It was my first time hearing that God could give all that grace. She told us her testimony and it touched me. Up until this point I did not know if I was going to hell or heaven, but I know I was trying to be a good person. All I knew was everything was a sin. That is how we were taught at the Pentecostal church. You could not wear makeup, nails, weave, short skirts, and even could not go to the movies because that was a sin. So, I always thought I was not good enough for God. But little did I know my deliverance was right around the corner.

That weekend we went to church and it was the last day of the encounter. I was full of joy and very emotional. During Sunday service they allowed all the kids to go on stage and tell our testimony, so they asked my sister Stacey and me could we tell our testimony and how the weekend impacted us. So, I went first to speak to about 2000 congregation. This was big for me because I never really talked. So, I pulled the courage together to tell the people how I would drink and party. Doing this just to take pain away and escape from reality. I told them how I prayed to God for him to send me some guidance or parents. As I was speaking, I asked my aunt and uncle to come up to the front. They were in tears and I began to thank them for all they had done for my sister Stacey and me. Little did I know that God changed the course of my life and allowed me to come to a home with loving guardians and a great support group in church.

The encounter had helped me with forgiveness. The years of abuse, molestation, abandonment, rejection, hurt, and pain. It was a start of change. The place where God met me and opened my eyes.

Prayer of Grace

God meets you where you are. The shackles of your past will not define or hold you back. The answer that you are looking for is right next door. God is about to go beyond your own thoughts. For God is a man of grace and mercy, his hands are upon you. So, in the mist of your trail favor is upon you and God is covering you. So, do not give up when it seems as if you do not have the answer to your problem. For God is faithful and he will never leave or forsake you.

Leadership Team

During this time Stacey and I had made some friends at church. They became our closest friends. I remember one of them writing me a letter and asking did I want to be in a ladies 12 group and that Mrs. Faith would mentor us. So, my sister jumped on board. I was happy I had a friend. A twelve group is just like the 12 disciples in the Bible. God gave them guidance and that is what Mrs. Faith did. She became a mentor, friend, sister, spiritual mother, and today my life coach. During this time, we joined a leadership team at the church. It was the 24 table that was led by teenagers. Our youth pastor at the time was Pastor Sunny and his wife Mrs. Sally. At the time I did not know that later Pastor Sunny would shape my whole life and become a spiritual father. On this leadership team we started to do encounters and to teach. At first, I was very shy, so I did not teach until I was 17. But I was 16 at the time when I joined the leadership team. My sister Stacey taught social life every encounter. I remember whishing I could do that and have more confidence like that. But little did I know my time was coming soon. So, my role was to lead small groups at the encounter. I was always nervous because we had to attend to about 300 young people at these encounters. But little did I know, God was preparing me for something great.

The next year my sister Stacey was a senior and she had to pick what college she was going to go to. Her decision was to move back to Louisiana and attend a college there. I remembered when she packed her bags and left. I was really hurt and sad. Once again, I felt abandoned. During this time, the Lord told me to stay in Oklahoma and to not go home. So, I stayed. Little did I know being away from my sister would really help me. I began to come out of my shyness. I was no longer in her shadow, so I had to stand alone a lot of times.

As time went on, I began to get more involved in church. By the age of 17, I was teaching sermons at encounters like my sister Stacey. She really motivated me to do this. I was now standing on my own discovering my own purpose. I began to figure out my spiritual gifts and began to operate in them. I began to really study my Bible and write sermons all the time. I looked forward to teaching and telling my testimony. But God was not finished with me, he was just getting started.

When my sister moved, I began to struggle in school badly. The kids at my school were more advanced than I was. My toughest class was math and the teacher really did not help me because there were too many students. Currently, I was 17 attending Broken Arrow Senior high. I was in the 10th grade. The school was so huge I had a hard time socially coping. So, one day my Uncle Jeff and Aunt Sue told me our church Greenwood Christian Center was starting a home school with 12 students. They were thinking about putting me and their daughter in the school. They said we are going to a meeting about it and do I want to go and see what it was about. I was a little nervous about being home schooled, but little did I know it would set me up for purpose. So, we went to the meeting and all my friends from church were there. So, I got excited and said of course I would go there. Now my teacher would be my pastor's wife Pastor Sally who later in life would step in and become like a spiritual mother.

I started the school in the 11th grade. My cousin and I attended the school for a year. We got to pick our own classes and I chose classes that were centered on government. We had different speakers that would come and speak to us. We also had cooking classes, which was fun. I also took piano lessons from a piano player who graduated from Julliard. But one of the most difficult things for me was going to counseling. My counselor really helped me out a lot and I got to tell her things I never told people. She became my big sister. She would come to my house and play video games with me and just chill with me, which was great for me because I needed a big sister at the time who would guide me. But the great thing about home school was that I graduated a year earlier than my expected date. A lot of people did not know I failed the second grade, so I was a grade behind. I always felt bad even when I got older, so when I graduated a year earlier God had answered my prayer. What that showed me is God remembers your prayers as a little girl and you may have to wait. God is preparing blessings for you.

Now during this time in home school, I got to know the Pastor Sally and Pastor Luke very well the head Pastors of Green Wood Christian Center. At the time I had made a close bond with their children. I began to stay some nights with them and when my Aunt Sue and Uncle Jeff left town. I really enjoyed going to them. Even though my life in church was not perfect in Mississippi. I felt like God was opening me up to their life to show me how pastors live with grace and pure love. Little did I know that this family would go above and beyond for me. In ways I do not think that a lot of people would do.

Chapter 4

The Struggle

As time went on, while I was doing great things and even teaching at church going to a great school, I was struggling on the inside. I was barely talking to my mother. My mother has been in and out of hospital because of health issues and I am fighting missing her while not knowing her condition. I felt as my mother had abandoned me so I had this void that I constantly dealt with daily. I often talked to God about it and I prayed a lot. Also, remember I am human so sometimes I felt mad or sometimes I tried to remember the happy times. I wondered did she want me. It was difficult living with my aunt and uncle because I needed a mom and dad. So, I did not always feel complete or felt rejected by them. I had a hard time talking to my aunt because I wondered sometimes did she really like me and I kind of did not want to give her the spot of being my mother because I felt like I would be letting go of my biological mother. But at the same time, I really wanted some parents and needed a lot of attention and love. I also know I had a lot of daddy issues. It was difficult being in the house with a man because majority of the time before I lived with him, I was being molested, physically and emotionally. So, I really felt like I could not be truly close to him because I had a fear of men.

Even though I felt that way about my aunt and uncle, I can honestly say they did nothing to harm me at all and I was well provided for. They showed me a different lifestyle that I could live, and that poverty is not an option for me. They opened doors for me by exposing me to a diverse culture, new adventures, traveling, and being a teenager. Also, they taught me how to be responsible and if you want something in life you have to really work for it in life. They showed me how Christians should be as people and they were involved in church which encouraged me and my sister to be involved. It is easy to follow Christ when you have great role models. I am not saying they are perfect by any means they had their problems and flaws. But they were real and honest and wanted the best for me. So, for that I thank them.

As a teenager I was often angry at them for different reasons. I was not getting enough attention and feeling left out or for feeling like a stepchild. But God has taught me how to forgive and look at the positive side. Sometimes God must change your perspective and order for you to be healed. I am not perfect, and it took a while for me to build a close relationship with them. Even to continue it as an adult. God is still working on me in some areas and I know it is always room for improvement whether I think I need it or not.

A Spiritual Bond

While I was living with my uncle and aunt. As I attended my new school my aunt and uncle would travel. While they would travel about a couple of times out of the week, I would go stay with Pastor Sally. She was my teacher, and I became close with her kids. Little did I know God was setting this relationship up for me to help me in areas in my life that I knew I needed guidance in. As I got to know pastor Sally, I learned a lot about her, and it even changed my perspective of white people. I often was scared to go over white people's houses afraid of what others would think of me or even wondered if they really liked black people. But pastor Sally did not see color. She just saw love, which broke down those racial barriers.

I remember while being in school I admired Pastor Sally. A lot of reason why I am who I am today is because Pastor Sally took time out to go the extra mile and invest in me. She often showed the human side of her and not the pastor side. Being all deep and spiritual. When I would talk to her about different things in my life, she never made me feel less than, and she was always good at keeping secrets.

One thing that I noticed about Pastor Sally and her husband Pastor Luke is they were people with integrity. They were always honest and transparent with things within their house even when it was difficult. I admired the way they showed a level of grace to their kids and to their congregation. I often wondered how they could deal with so many people and the stuff they faced at home. But I knew it was only because of God's grace that they could hold the capacity of the calling that God had on their lives. They did not know this, but I often prayed for them when things were going on and even when things were going well. I learned that it is important to pray for your spiritual leaders because you never know what they are facing. These pastors also helped heal my perspective of ministers and not looking at people as perfect and that God is the only one perfect. Pastor Sally was a true blessing and blessed my life in ways that she did not know she did at a young age.

Community College

As time went on, I ended up graduated homeschool a year early. It was a great accomplishment. I was supposed to take 6 classes just to complete the 11th grade. But I ended up taking 12 classes and completing two grades in one year. I did not know I had done this until Pastor Sally told me you have taken enough classes to graduate. One thing that I did was when I finished one course I was interested in, I just moved to another course. I never tried to complete so many classes at one time. I just found courses that I was interested in and I was glued to my computer screen. One thing that God does not give us is time. I have learned how to value it and to be productive with it. Homeschool was preparing me for college because a lot of times teachers do not teach you everything and you must be independent and learn it on your own. One thing that I will always take with me and that Pastor Sally taught me is to set goals for your day every day. Now that may seem small to many people but because I have done that, I have been able to make small and big goals for my life and I have accomplished them. Having daily goals and life goals is a key to your success for the present and for the future.

One goal that I wanted to accomplish was to go to college. So, Pastor Sally helped this dream come true. I really did not have a lot of guidance and education going into the college process. I lacked a lot of understanding. I had a 3.8 and did not even know that I could go anywhere I wanted and just settled to go to a community college. My dream was to go to Harvard, but I had a lot of fears and was scared to spread my wings. I had gotten letters from other colleges and did not realize how big of a deal it was because I did not really have that support team cheering me on to go off and do big things. The only person who I felt was cheering me on was Pastor Sally, so I went to a community college off a two-year scholarship.

As I entered community college, I was excited. I beat the odds of what everyone thought I would be. I knew that I was starting a new path. But I was scared because I did not know what I wanted to do. I just knew college was a start, and there was no turning back. A lot of people did not realize I was overcoming a lot going to college. From being kicked out of class as a young girl because of my temper. To having a speech problem and having a hard time talking. Lastly, overcoming a lot of trauma as a kid. I knew that God had my back and that I could overcome anything.

As I was in community college, I continued to go to Pastor Sally's and Pastor Luke's house. Pastor Sally kind of helped me keep a leveled head and to stay on top of my work and school. She was the one person who believed in me. During this time in college, I tried to maintain going to church, but I was not involved because of my commitment to school. But I knew I was doing the right thing.

But as I went to school, I had a lot of challenges emotionally, mentally, and health wise. I missed my family a lot and often felt as if I had left my family because I had chosen a path that many had not traveled. I picked a college far from home and did not return home. My mother was sick, and I was not by her side. But the only thing I kept telling myself was that it was going to be worth it once I cross that stage and get that degree, so I had to keep the faith and not let doubt creep in.

As time went on, I started to not do good in school. I was taking classes that were not credited because I had to test on a certain level because I was homeschooled. So, I felt like going to a community college was a waste of time and money. I felt less than because I could not get certain test scores. At the time I did not have a car, so

I was walking to school up the street from my house, so I was really stressed. My health started to go downhill.

While I was walking to school one day my chest began to tighten up and I fell on the side of the sidewalk. I began to have an anxiety attack because my stress level was so high. I never told anyone I was having the attacks because I did not know what they were until I went to the doctor. They told me I had high blood pressure at a young age, I had asthma, and was having anxiety attacks. I had lost so much weight. All this was going on while I was staying with my aunt and uncle. They knew a little about my health but not to this extent, so I kept it to myself. Until I was on the phone with my sister and had an asthma attack. I had to be open and tell her some of my health issues. But I did not tell her everything because she lived in another state and I did not want her to worry.

Two years had gone by and I was still in community college and my health was getting worse. During this time, I believe depression had kicked in, but I did not know it. I would barely sleep through the night. I was having bad back pains where every night I would sleep on my floor because of stress. I would wake up throughout the night having asthma attacks and crying. A lot of times I felt hopeless and alone. At the time it was getting hard. Often, I would try to go to Pastor Sally's house to escape from my problems or to my mentor's house Mrs. Faith. She always would let me stay at her house weeks at a time and would talk me to sleep. I would go to Mrs. Faith's house because I felt a level of peace at her house and I could get a good night rest. When I went to her house, I never had asthma attacks or anxiety attacks. Mrs. Faith brought a light to many dark places in my life. She always told me no matter what do not give up and quit.

She would tell me you are going to get your degree. Just stay on the course and in due time it will come to pass.

My second year of community college had gone by. I was with Mrs. Faith one day after school. I received a phone call from one of my uncles that my aunt in Louisiana that helped raise me died. I started to scream when I got off the phone. I was devasted. She had died from sickle cell disease. I felt bad because I was not visiting home like I should. She was like a mother figure to me and I felt like I had lost my best friend. It hurt my soul. But I knew life had to go on. So, I held this in and never talked or dealt with it until years later because it hurt so much.

Grief Prayer

I pray that if someone has lost a loved one and have been impacted. That God is coming to your rescue. I have faith that he will heal that wound and God will mend your heart. As much as you feel that you have lost that it will be given back to you. We may not understand what God does. But know it is in the best interest of us. God works in mysterious ways. So, let God do his work. So, I pray that his grace and mercy cover the loved ones who have gone on to be with him.

Chapter 5

Goodbye to Making a Change

As I was attending Tulsa Community College there was a huge shift that was coming my way. One day I came in the house and sat at the dinner table. My Aunt Sue was in the kitchen cleaning and cooking. While my Uncle Jeff came to sit at the table with me. My aunt began to tell me that they were moving to Dallas in a couple of months. My uncle really did not say anything, and I was very shocked. She told me I need to get a plan and basically get it together soon.

As an 18-year-old I was devasted. Many people would say you are 18 years old it is time for you to move out and find your own way. But immediately I started hurting because it was not said we are going to move all together it was them. So, those abandonment issues started to kick in. I felt lost again. I believe this happened because I often moved from home to home at a young age. The adults that would take care of me where like temporary people. My mother was in and out of my life as a teenager because she had her own issues. My birth father never raised me and was never around. So, I sucked it up and said ok I must figure it out. I said I guess this is adulthood. But I knew I did not have it all together. I was working a minimum wage job. I was having a lot of health issues. So, I knew I needed some help.

The next day I went to Pastor Sally and Pastor Luke's house. I waited until we were alone one night in the car. I began to tell Pastor Sally my aunt and uncle was moving away and that I needed a place to stay. It almost felt embarrassing to ask her. But she did not ask any questions and just smiled. She said let me talk to Pastor Luke. Now this may of seem easy for some people. But it was difficult for me because I knew going back to Louisiana was not an option for me because I was still in school and I thought it was a bad idea. Also, I felt a strong connection with the church I had been attending. During this time, I was not open to my family about this because I wanted my transition to be peaceful. I did not want to hear their opinions. Now I think if my aunt that died was alive. I think the story would have been a little different. But I think everything worked out for the good even though I would face many challenges.

A couple of weeks went by and my legal guardians were moving out of their home. I moved ahead of time into my pastor's home. Now I tell you I was nervous to live with them. But they welcomed me with open arms. Pastor Sally told me they were redecorating their son's old room. They went above and beyond to make me feel as if I was family. They treated me no different than their kids. I remember watching them do my room and asking me my input. For some reason, all that had made me feel overwhelmed. Not with sadness but with tears of joy. I remember laying in my new room my first night, crying. I was thanking God that I had certain people in my corner that would help me. I soon told my family that I had moved with them. But it took me a while because I did not want anything to change my mind.

Step Out on Faith

I would say for the people who are questioning some of the decisions that you have done. If you believe what God has told you.

Do not second guess yourself. It may not look like the best decisions and we may not know what God is trying to do in that hour. But trust him and stand on his word for that college, job, business plan, or anything else. Just trust him and not yourself.

Hearing God on Going to Oral Roberts University

About a year had gone by and I knew it was time to leave the community college. Right before my uncle and aunt have left, I received a letter from Oral Roberts University. That was my dream college I wanted to go to, but I was nervous. I felt as if I could not afford it. But I kept thinking about it and it kept being laid on my heart to go there.

So, I finally got the courage and told Pastor Sally that was the college I wanted to go to. But I still did not know how that was going to happen. So, Pastor Sally said we are going to believe God for the money and walk in faith. We went to the school and talked to financial aid I had got some aid but the rest I had to pray it through and finally I had received the rest of my aid.

But I can remember every year I was believing God and not knowing was I going to go back to school. I can think back on times I was short on tuition and Pastor Sally and Pastor Luke making up the difference and even getting my schools books for me. Many times financially it was very tough. I spent 5 years in undergraduate school because of so many obstacles I faced.

I can remember being scared to ask Pastor Sally and Pastor Luke's help. I was $500 short of my tuition or they were going to kick me out of school. So, I went home for school break and told my grandma ahead of time before I got home. I went to Louisiana to my grandma's for break and my last day. She said baby do you still owe money and I said yes. She pulled out an envelope and began to count a whole lot of money and told me to put out my hand. She counted out $500 and I was in tears. I did not know where she got all that money, but I was in tears. At this moment I said I must graduate because she is investing and believing in me. My grandma even bought a lot of groceries for me and two friends that I drove there with. They were grateful. That is one memory I will never forget about my grandma. She believed in me even when it was hard to believe in myself.

Now I know many people are asking where is your aunt and uncle? During this time, I did not ask them for anything. I did not even go visit them often. Imagine most of your life feeling like a burden to others. Or having feelings or abandonment and rejection. Those where some of the things I was going through. So, I decided I would not ask them for anything. Now those were previous issues I was dealing with before I lived with them. For a person with a mindset like that it is hard to ask for things.

So, I would spend many holidays and birthdays with my pastors. Even though I was spending time with them I often thought of my family. But I could not afford to go home sometimes. I figured if I asked, I would not get what I wanted. I thought like that because of childhood experiences. I had later moved on campus going to college. But I would go to the pastors' house every weekend because I enjoyed their company. One thing I do have to say is this family never turned me away. I am grateful for all they did from the quality time, talks, holidays, and expenses. Not taking credit from my family. But the bible says give honor where honor is due.

Prayer of Gratitude

After this passage, my heart is full. I would like to thank everyone who has helped me along the way. God has changed my perspective and views on a lot of things. Many people along the way and family and friends did not have to step in and care for me. A lot of things I did not understand at a young age. But I now understand. A lot of things were done for the betterment of my life and future. I learned do not always look at the negative but the positive in every situation and do not forget where God has brought you from. No matter how high and low God takes you in life. So, I thank you to everyone and especially to God for taking me through. But for mostly bringing me out.

Chapter 6
Oral Roberts University Experience

While I was at Oral Roberts University, I really enjoyed my time there. I ended up on a floor with some amazing girls. Our floor was the floor everyone loved to come to. We had built a bound that that was priceless. We all would go to class and it was like a party on our floor. We would come together around 5 p.m. to eat together. We talked about our day and often ate together with our brother dorm. At ORU we always had chapel so I basically would go to chapel twice a week. I enjoyed services and the little community of friends there.

While at ORU I got to experience some things at the school that I would not change. My second year there I got the opportunity to go to Puerto Rico. Instead of taking my Spanish class I got the opportunity to travel and receive class credit that way. I never would have thought in a million years that I would get a chance to do that. I met some amazing people there and made some friends that went on the trip with me. While there I also had to work and I did not have a problem with that. I had to read a book and write a 10-page paper in 4 hours in front of the teacher about the book. This was not easy. But somehow, I got an A plus grade. One memory I will not forget about the trip is the culture there. I learned and studied a lot about the culture there. The food was amazing as well. One thing I remember that will always stay with me. Is going to the mall there and I went into a store. I forgot that they spoke Spanish and started speaking English. I asked her how much some pants were. She dropped her head and told me in Spanish she did not know English. So, I tried to ask her in Spanish, and she laughed. She then told me in Spanish. This little moment taught me so much. We both had a language barrier. But we both tried to come down on each other's level to understand each other's language and cultures. Just because someone is different than you, it does not mean they are less than. We all can learn from someone else.

College Shift

As three years have gone by at college. Things began to change a lot. Some people that I met moved on and others dropped out of school. I went from having roommates to having my own room the rest of college. As time went on, I would study for long hours and started to get like 3 or 4 hours a sleep. I was doing my work and helping other students at the same time. Little did I know I began to get stressed and get sick often. I started to lose a lot of hair. I could remember me waking up for class and finding hair laying in my bed. I did not know what was going on. This should have been a sign for me to slow down and reach out to people to see what was going on with my health.

I remember one day I was in my room and I started having flashbacks about my past. Different things that happened to me. I felt as if my trauma that I had never dealt with was bothering me. Currently, I was barely sharing things or talking to family about my health. Then I started waking up to class late and sleeping in class. Little did I know my professors started to notice the change. My favorite professor was watching me at the time and he later reached out to my academic advisor and told her about the way I was acting in class. I knew something was wrong, so I went to the school nurse and they told me to go to another place to get checked out. But I thought they were looking at me like I was going crazy, so I stopped going to them. As time went on, I tried to hide my health problems, but they began to show. Now at this point my Chaplin reached out to me to see if she could help me because she was notified that something may be wrong with me. I stopped going to chapel and stopped going to class. It got to the point where I could not focus in class. I was experiencing things that made me nervous to be around people. So, I kept to myself. It got to the point where the head person of the women's dorm came to me and suggested I needed a roommate and asked the girls on my floor to reach out to me. But I kept my distance and did not seek help. Little did I know I started to have mental health problems, and this was a start of something that I could not stop and that I would not wish upon my worst enemy.

Leaving Campus

One day I was at my pastor's house and Pastor Sally asked did I want to move in, and I told her yes. I knew that I was having health problems and did not want to be on campus. But this would only lead me into a darker place. While I was staying at Pastors Sally's house. I started to deal with not being able to sleep at night. So, what I would do was sleep throughout the day and stay up all night. There would be times where I would go a couple of days without sleep. During that time, I just thought I dealt with bad nerves. It got to the point where I was so paranoid to go to class, I stopped going. But I did not tell anyone. This was the beginning stage of anxiety and paranoia. At the time I did not know. I would try to hide it, but I could tell the people around me knew something was wrong. As time went on, I stopped hanging with a lot of my friends and lost my social life because I started to be fearful to engage with people. As things began to get worse, I started to fall into a dark depression. I did not know this at the time, but this was the name of something that would begin to haunt me. I can remember sometimes getting in my car and driving around for hours because I was paranoid.

I remember one day I woke up and I was very irritable, and something said you must get out of here before you get worse. I believe God was telling me that you need to go get help. So, I went downstairs and told my Pastors that I wanted to take a trip home out of the blue and that I needed to do something at school. At the time I could feel the inside of my body wanting to burst out into a rage. I started to feel anger, and no one had done anything to me. I knew this was not normal. I started to feel as if as I was having a mood swing that was coming up like a temper. Immediately I knew I did not want them to see that side of me. I felt like I was about to do something or hurt someone and it was out of my will power. So, I packed my bags and got on the bus to go to Texas with a one-way ticket.

Mental Health Is Real

I would advise anyone who has gone through any mental health problems to seek help. Never try to hide something that will only get worse in the long run. At the time I was hiding it because of the bad stigma, and I did not want to be diagnosed with something. I have learned that not everything that happens with mental health is your fault. Maybe it comes from trauma, circumstances, or even DNA. Overtime I have had to learn that I am not less than because I have gone through this and do not blame myself. I would encourage people to know it is wise to be aware of your mental health and to seek help and support. One nugget that I would love to leave with everyone is that God still loves you no matter what state of mind you are in or what you have gone through.

Chapter 7

Transition to Texas

Little did I know Texas was going to be my home for a year and I was not going to return to school yet. When I came to Texas my mother's brother and sister were living there. At the time I was staying with my sister and my mother and brother were staying there as well. When I arrived, I did not tell my family that I felt like something was wrong with me. But they will soon find out. I started to feel sick while I was at my sister's. I started to sleep all day on the couch and not really talk to anyone. Then I started to have nightmares every night and seeing things that were not there, which later I found out were hallucinations. It got to the point where I had to sleep with my mom every night because I was scared to sleep by myself. I can remember me sleep and was having a nightmare and my mom shaking me out of my sleep to let me know I was alright. It got to the point where I was fearful to go to sleep. At the time I probably should have gone to the doctor, but I did not. This behavior started to get worse. I started to hallucinate while awake and would just sit until they would go away.

One day I remember me going into the kitchen and going into a rage and I grabbed something and tried to throw it. My mother grabbed it out of my hand. Then I took a glass picture off the wall and slammed it to the ground and broke it into pieces. I was basically going into rages that I could not control. I believe I was a danger to myself and to others.

Somehow, I was able to call Pastor Sally because I needed help. At the time when I called, I barely could get my words out because I became incoherent. To this day I only can remember bits and pieces of this conversation because I was so out of it. She knew something was wrong with me and immediately started to worry. It only got worse.

Later that night, I went into the restroom and I started to swing my fist in the air. I thought I was fighting someone. It had really got crazy many religious people would say it was demonic. So, I really did not tell anyone ever in my life about this day. I started screaming in the restroom and my mom ran to the restroom. But the door was locked, and she kept telling me to unlock the door because she knew something was wrong. But suddenly, I tried to reach for the lock. As I was reaching to unlock the door, I passed out and fell to the floor. I went headfirst down first and hit my jaw on the side of the sink and fell into the hallway as the door opened from me grabbling it. My mother began to call my name. But my speech was slurred, and I was incoherent. My mother called for my sister on the phone. She rushed over and helped me off the floor and they brought me to her boyfriend's house. Then they finally decided that I needed to go to the hospital. When I got there, I could not remember anything that happened. I just knew my jaw hurt and I felt very weird. The next day I remember that Pastor Sally was at the hospital. She was in town with some other women from the church. It was God because she was in town for something and her hotel was right across the street from me. I really could not say anything to her because I did not know what was going on. I was very scared at the hospital because the doctors were doing things I did not understand.

Felt Like Prison

The next day they finally released me. But as I was being rolled out, I saw a cop car and the police told me to get in the back seat. Now there was another woman in the back car, and she was handcuffed. I looked at my mom as she smiled and walked off. The first thing I thought was what the hell is going on. Fear came upon me. I could not remember if I hurt someone. No one explained anything to me. So, I was in the back of this car and he began to drive for about a two-hour drive. I remember just seeing land and trees. The lady in the back with me was talking to herself. I remember her asking the police officer to stop so she could use the restroom and she was about to go to the bathroom in the car. I was like thinking in my head please do not pee in this car with me back here.

So, we finally got to one stop and it was a prison. I started to think oh God what did I do. But we just stopped to get food there and to drop her off at the prison. I got back into the car and we started to drive some more. The last thing I remember was walking down a long hallway and me entering through a gate and being placed in a bed to go to sleep. From my understanding, I went to sleep and was on so much medication at this place I had slept so much a week went by and did not even know it. I can remember waking up one day and starting to realize I was in a hospital that was a place for people who were having mental illness like myself. At first, I thought I was in prison when I came to myself. The place was caged off from the public. There were different units that people lived in. There were staff that watched you all day and there was a glass window where doctors and staff watched you. You had to meet with a doctor and go to classes to help you get better. I had three other women in my room and I feared them. One girl would talk to herself throughout the night. These people where strangers and I did not want to get to know them. For a while, many nights where scary for me. There were people who came to our room at night to make sure everyone was sleep. While I was there for the first couple of weeks I stayed in my room and did not talk at all. I only came out to eat and got up to take medication and would sleep throughout the day.

Staff at the Hospital

I met my doctor for the first time, and he told me that I stayed in my room too much. He said the sooner I get better the sooner I could go home. So, I started to work out while I was in there. Then I started to go to life skill classes and come out of my room. Then a man from the staff started to fall in love with me as I came back to normal. I still could barely remember anything. But I started to face troubles while I was in there. I started to get bullied by two staff members. I can remember one staff member stopped waking me up to get meds and breakfast and I started to be rude to her to let her know she could not bully me. Another was not letting me take a bath. I asked her could I take a bath after all the women took a bath because I was scared to bathe with a lot of women I did not know. I was trying to be cautious because how the staff and patients were there. I did not want anything sexual to happen to me while I was there. So, she started skipping my time to take a bath. This was her way of bullying me. So, one day she laughed in my face and I charged at her and tried to punch her in the face. A man grabbed me and pinned me down. Then next time I talked to my doctor, I found out the reason why I was still in there was because they thought I had not learned how to bathe myself again. But she was skipping over me to take a bath, so I told my doctor. He said thank you for telling me. But there were a couple of staff who started to look out for me. One lady that was Vietnamese she became my friend. She said anything that happens to me let me know. She started bringing me food from home and we got close. Then other staff would take me behind the glass, and we would talk for hours about life. They finally saw that I was normal. After a while I started to get better.

My family finally started to visit me. My mom, sister, and grandmother would often come see me. When I saw them, I knew there was hope and I was doing better. It made me feel like they cared because at first, I thought they threw me away into this facility with crazy people. It gave me motivation to do better and be active so I could go home.

As time went on, I started to experience things in this facility and see a lot. I can remember one lady. It was dinner time, and I was at my table and there was a white lady at another table. She was looking at me like she was about to do something. So, I grabbed my tray and fork because I knew she had impulsive behavior. One of the staff saw that there was a lot of silent tension between me and the lady and he sat between us. He looked at me and said I got you. Then within seconds the lady jumps up and says you Niger and she grabbed a sharp object. The man jumped up and told me to leave. I just walked off and smiled at her. I knew she had problems, so I left her alone.

Another incident happened when I was in line going to eat. This man started to pick on me. He was standing with his girlfriend and she was a muscular Hispanic lady. Her boyfriend pushed her into me and said fight her. I looked at the lady and was looking like please do not do this because I do not want to have to fight in here. But I knew that I was not going to let something happen to myself. So, the lady told her boyfriend no I am not going to hit her. I was trying to stay out of trouble.

So, about a month and a couple of weeks went by and I met with the doctor. He said it was time to go home. He mentioned I have made a full recovery and that I was in a good mental state. He saw that I had a strong family support that I could go home to because my mom, sister, and grandma came to visit often. So, I finally returned home.

Chapter 8

Returning Home

My last day at the facility was one of the best days of my life. The doctor told me a week earlier that I would be returning home and that I had done a good job. I made a complete recovery and was back to myself. I will never forget when I got on the van to go home. I said to myself I will never get back to this low place in my life ever again. This was a dark place I would not wish for anyone. I also started to thank God that I had my health back.

When I got out the van and knocked on my sister's door, I was greeted with joy. Words could not express how I felt in that moment. When I got out of the van everyone in the van said take care of yourself. I took it as you are a good person do not come back to this place and stay healthy.

In this moment of returning home, I needed time to spend with my family. Just to talk to my mom, sister, and brother really helped me out. Now coming from the facility kind of made me feel like I just got out of prison. I had not heard from some of my friends and I would soon find out that many of my friends would leave my side. Others would be really concerned because I disappeared with no warning.

My transition to coming home was a little different. My brother would be the one who would take care of me until I got back on my feet. I will never forget how he catered to me every day. He made sure I was taking care of myself and was eating. He even tried to help find me a job. I really had not seen this side of him before. As time went on, I realized I needed to do something with my life and that my dark place was just a setback.

During this time in my free time, I started to do a lot of selfcare. I started to pick up my pen and started back writing music and poems. I did this all day. I believe when you go through something like that it would take some time to process what a person has gone through. It became difficult for me to explain to people why I went missing. So, I tried to avoid the conversation with people who would ask where I had been. I had not accepted that I struggled with mental health. It would take years for me to accept my struggles and problems that I would face in the future. To me it was still embarrassing to let people know that side of me.

Self-Esteem

As time went on, I started to struggle with my self-esteem. I started to feel less of myself because of what I had gone through. I did not realize that I would go through this after coming home. I often thought man I am not normal. I questioned whether I could live a normal life at all. I knew a lot of people did not accept a person with issues like mine. At this point in my life, I was 23 and I worried about what people thought of me. As I looked back over my life, I felt like most of my 20's I struggled mentally with a lot. But one thing I started to do that really helped was to work out. I noticed when I worked out it made me feel good about myself.

As I had problems with my self-esteem, my confidence was not in a good place. I started to shy back and not really want to be around people. I always wondered could people see something was wrong with me. I started to hate to be around people and wanted to keep to myself. I think when you go through something like what I had gone through, you should have an outlet to express yourself and to process your emotions. I jumped back into society and tried to burry what I had gone through. Me and my family did not talk about it. We kind of just picked up where I left off and moved forward the best way we knew how to.

While I was dealing with my self- esteem problems and trying to gain my confidence back. I still said to myself I want to make something out of myself and that I was not going to be a failure.

Confidence Pray

I pray for anyone who is dealing with self-esteem issues. Know that you are wonderful and fearfully made. I would encourage you to do things that you love. Go back to the kid that dreamed again. I pray that you have a support team that would surround you with love. But the best love you will experience is God. He will wipe your tears away and restore your self-image. Never give up on your purpose and what God has called you to be. Remember the joyous days which will outweigh the bad days. May God be with you in the darkest days as well as your bright days.

Back on Track

One day I was at my sister's place laying on the couch and I heard a voice say. It is time for you to get up and go back to school. I opened my eyes and thought I do not even know if I am going to be able to get back into school because I dropped out of school. I am sure I lost my scholarships and would they let me back into this school. That same voice told me to stop worrying and just start doing. So, a couple of days passed by and I finally made the decision to go back. I told my sister, mother, and brother. They were happy that I had the confidence to try and go back. I knew I could not give up that easy.

I finally called the school and got a hold of some people. They told me I could come back to school. They told me I could get on a payment plan to pay for my education. Now about a year had gone by during this time. But I did not care I just wanted my degree. I had two more semesters to complete and something in me knew that I could do it. The school was great at making sure I had everything. They also told me because I dropped out of school I would have to be on academic probation and that I had to keep my GPA at a certain score. The school also suggested that I go to the school counselor once a week. I did not care what I had to do to get back into school. I knew this was a God thing because everything had worked out fine. This was a new beginning for me.

Chapter 9

Finish What I Started

When I finally made my decision to go back to college, I called Pastor Sally to let her know I was coming back and going back to school. She was extremely excited that I decided to go back, and I did not give up. But one thing that I did want to change was my living environment. Nothing was wrong with Pastor Sally's house. I just felt that I needed to stay on campus to stay focused. I also did not want a roommate. I thought this would be great because I needed my own private space. I knew this time around things were going to be better. Also, because I was aware of my health problems, I could take care of myself. I learned that it is important to be aware of your health before a doctor or hospital make you aware. I did not want anything that I experienced to happen again.

Back on Campus

When I arrived back on campus things where a little different. A lot of people that I had known had dropped out or graduated. The hardest thing I had to deal with was the people who knew me on campus and some of my friends wanted to know what happened to me. Because I fell off the face of the earth. I told all my friends that I went to stay with my family. Some of them I had to apologize to because they thought that they did something wrong. I felt as if I should keep my health and personal life to myself.

As I started going to my classes, I started to really get back into the swing of things and really enjoy school again. I kind of kept to myself a lot of times and kept a small group of people around me that I knew would keep me positive and support me with some of my goals and graduating. One major support that I had was from my teacher. Because I was on academic probation, I had to meet with my academic advisor every week to tell her my grades and to talk about classwork. When I tell you, this lady knew everything about my classes. Trust me she knew every bit. Many students would have hated this amount of accountability. But I loved it because it showed me that she cared. She was a nice lady, but she did not play when it came down to my grades. If I missed a day of class she would know, and my teachers would be emailing me. Sometimes it takes accountability like that to get you to the next phase of your life or to accomplish a goal.

When I returned to school, I also had to start seeing a counselor. It really was not something I wanted at first. But it helped me express my feelings. At this time, I did not want anyone to know I was going to the school counselor, so I kept it to myself. I only went to her just for a semester then stopped. After I thought I could do it by myself.

Maintaining Health

As a couple of months went by, I was in good health. But one thing I was concerned about was my weight. I had gained so much weight that I could not fit any more of my clothes. So, I asked my sister could she buy me some more clothes. To me this was so embarrassing. I had to throw out all my old clothes. Many people told me I looked healthier with my weight gain. But I knew I did not like it. One thing that it had taken me a while to say is I am going to try and love myself the way I am. I thought it is better to be healthy and in my right mind than skinny and losing my mind!

At that time, I was doing good. My health was back on track and my social life was ok. I was just more focused on graduating and staying out of the hospital. At this point I would say I was learning how to take care of myself. As an adult you can be doing unhealthy things or somethings can be going on with a person's body and the person continues to ignore the signs. I have learned God sends signs and warnings for you to recognize. But it is our job to act and take care of ourselves once we know these things. A lot of things I did not know and was not educated in some of these areas. Especially things that were concerning mental health. Even though I was aware of my health issues, it would take years for me to accept some of my issues and to be open about them. But I still would take care of myself because I was scared to go back into those dark places I had once gone to.

Lack of Faith

As time went on, I would still go to Pastor Sally's and Pastor Luke's house. I would go to their house often when I had free time. But one thing I noticed about myself that I was not telling them or my friends, I was losing faith in God a little. It started to become hard for me to go to church. I noticed that about me when I got out of the hospital before I moved back to Oklahoma. I started to think what I did wrong God to carry some of these mental burdens. A lot of people would not be this transparent with you but I am. I thought a lot about what I could have done so bad that these things would happen to me. So, I was trying to backtrack everything I had done and could not think of anything. As time went on and I would receive different doctors' reports, it was kind of killing my faith. So, I did not tell anyone.

Another area that hit my faith was my last semester at Oral Roberts University. I owed the school money and they said if I did not come up with the money I could not graduate. So, while my faith was being tested, I got down on my knees and prayed. God, I know you did not bring me this far to give up on me now. One thing that I did know was no matter if I had a church house or not. My mother taught me how to be a praying woman. That is one trait I have I think that got me through my tough days. So, when I prayed God gave me three names and I heard him clearly. God said ask those three people for the money. I did what he said and my remaining balance for that semester was paid off a week before me walking across that stage.

Chapter 10
The Big Day Graduation

The big day had finally come and I was filled with joy. Many people would have given up. But I knew that I was going to get that degree. It took me six years to get to the finish line. At first, I was ashamed to tell people it took me that long to finish school. But many people who have gone through similar situations like me overtime I have learned that they would have given up. I saw a lot of my friends come and go. Through not having enough money to finish school. Them not applying themselves or other circumstances.

I remember like it was yesterday. I was extremely nervous to walk across that stage, but I did. My Aunts, Uncle, Mom, and sister came from out of town for the big day. I could hear my family screaming from the stands. I could really hear my Mom's sister my Aunt screaming. As I crossed the stage I was almost in tears because I accomplished a goal that some days I thought would never happen. But the support over the years from family and my church family really got me to the other side.

After my graduation Pastor Sally and Pastor Luke threw me a graduation party. I loved every bit of it. Many of my friends showed up and surprised me. I really did not reach out to a lot of people. I just was happy my family showed up and that I got my degree. This was a moment in my life that I will always look back on and will not take the people who helped me out for granted. I know I put in most of the work, but I believe you never forget the people who helped you along the way.

Words of Encouragement Prayer

I would like to give some words of encouragement to anyone who is trying to accomplish a goal in life. Never give up on your dreams. No matter how long it takes you will get there. God is on your side and he will help you through it. Whether it's school or a business, you can accomplish the goal. It just takes a lot of hard work to get where you want to be in life. Never let someone tell you different. Especially if they have never walked a mile in your shoes.

Transition Back to the Real World

I graduated in 2014 from Oral Roberts University. Many people asked what I was going to do after I graduated. At that point I was happy I graduated. I do not think I knew what I wanted to do at that time. As months went on, I started to kind of feel impatient because I was not getting any jobs in my field. I moved back in with Pastor Sally and Pastor Luke. I knew I needed a job at the time because I was having car problems and I needed to pay off some things. Now this is a stage of my life. I was young in my twenty's. I would suggest to anyone just leaving college to seek out guidance. As I look back on this, I wish I would have reached out to my Uncle Jeff and Aunt Sue. I think I let my emotions get in the way or probably pride. A lot of times I did not want to be a burden to someone else. But one thing my sister taught me while I was in college was that closed mouths do not get fed. Meaning you will not get your needs met unless you open your mouth and ask.

Around this time my car that was used started to break down. I was so frustrated with this car. So, Pastor Luke and Pastor Sally were always coming to my rescue and they got my car fixed. They were always going that extra mile to make sure I had what I needed.

Seeking the Voice of God

As time went on, I started to really seek God's voice. Things were not going as good for me. I was struggling to find a job and I had a car that was not at its best. So, I finally wrote down about three states that I wanted to live in. I wrote down my pros and cons for each state. I felt peace about this move and decided to move to Houston, Texas. At the time my mom, brother, and sister were living there. I also had other family that lived there. This was another big step that I was going to have to make. I often went back and forth in my head about moving because I was scared to step out on my own. But I finally pulled myself together and told Pastor Sally and Pastor Luke my decision. They were incredibly happy for me and agreed that it would be a good move.

Despite the way I felt I knew I needed a change. It was time to step out on my own and not to let fear hold me back. I told my family in Texas I was moving back, and I had been talking to my sister for a while about it. They were happy and thought it was best for me.

Chapter 11
Minor Obstacles to Texas

In 2015 I decided to move to Houston, Texas. I felt like I needed a change. My mother, brother, and sister where living there and some other family members. So, I felt that being with my family would be good for my mental health. But the journey that I would take there only left me with more obstacles to face. Those small obstacles made me stronger and braver.

As I got on the road to Texas, I was extremely nervous. Mainly because I had never driven that far before. I only knew how to get there by navigation. Also, my pastors had just gotten my car out of the shop and I did not know if it would really get to Texas.

I loaded up my car early that morning and got on the road. I said Lord if you want me to go, then I must walk by faith and just get on this road. It was about a seven to eight-hour drive. So, while on this trip, I drove nonstop without stopping except for gas. But one stop I did make was to meet my mom in Dallas to help me drive the rest of the way to Houston. I am glad that she rode the rest of the way with me because complications came later down the road. I turned on my gospel music and prayed the entire way there. But as soon as I entered the state of Texas on the outside of Houston, I was about 15 minutes from my sister's place and my engine light came on. I was like oh lord please let my car make it.

Suddenly, my car started to jerk, and my mom said pull over. We stopped at a gas station and a man offered to help us. But he was asking for money. So, we said we were going to try and keep on driving. Since it was so late in the night and we were two women at that. Finally, my car stopped going and before it stopped on me, I pulled off the interstate. As soon as we pulled over another man stopped to check if we were all right. He was asking for food as well. I was like God please do not let us get robbed because it was not a nice part of town. We gave the man some food and he waited with us for a little while. I called my sister, and she was on her way.

My sister finally pulled up 15 minutes later. I was so happy to see her face that I was almost in tears. I was happy I made it. We called a tow truck and brough the car to my sister's place. The ride to Texas was a faith drive and a trip I will never forget.

Use Wisdom

As time went on, I started to adjust to the new state. A couple of months in I got my car fixed. As I started my new journey, I had finally gotten a job as a teacher and I loved my job. It was not the best pay, but it was a good start. I was happy I was on my feet and it felt good working. For me, a job helped build skills and confidence. I was able to work on this job for two years while I was in Texas.

Also, I started to go to church again. But one thing I stopped was going to see my doctors and keeping up with my health. I stopped doing what my doctors said and thought I got God I am going to do this on my own. I started doing this my last year at my job. A couple of months before I had to quit.

I can remember having a hard time sleeping. My sister slept in my room and told me to put on music. But I could not stop the voices and sounds I was hearing. I was shacking, being cold and hot because I was not on my meds. I was not watching tv because I thought the tv was talking to me. I was going through various things that were challenging for me. While this was going on, I was still managing to work.

One day I was at work and something did not seem right. I started to go through some things mentally that I would not wish upon anyone. I started to see things and hallucinate. I knew I was not safe to be around the kids and needed to get home. During this time, I also was struggling with anxiety and with other things that I could not handle. I ended up going home early that day. My boss was not happy, but she also knew I had medical problems. I went home and I started to feel dizzy. I ended up passing out for a little bit and coming to myself. I called my mom and could not get words out, I was incoherent. I started to scream and cry. Then I called my sister and she said dial 911. I finally called them, and they kept me on the phone until the ambulance pulled up. They asked me what was wrong, but I did not know. But I knew it had to do with my mental health. They asked me could I go upstairs and get my identification. As soon as I got up to get it as I approached the stairs, the room began to spin. I told them I was fine, and they could leave me. They told me no and said lady you are in a bad condition and we cannot leave you here. So, I went with them after I argued with them.

When I arrived at the hospital, they put me on a lot of medication and fluids. The doctors also put me to sleep because I would not listen to them. When my sister and mom arrived, I was much better. The doctor said you light up when you get with family. You are like an angel because I would not listen to the doctors at first. They told me I cannot go cold turkey and not take medicine and not listen to my doctors. I learned my lesson and it was my last time I did that. The doctor also suggested that I stop being a teacher because the environment was not good for my health. This right here hit hard. Mostly because I knew how hard it took to get the job. Also, I did not want to be statistics of a person with an illness that could not maintain a job. That was always a big fear for me. So, I had to just get out of my way and listen. I learned that sometimes God gives other people wisdom in areas that can benefit you in the future. This situation was a lesson for me.

First Campaign

A couple of months had gone by and I really wanted to do something in my major Government. So, the campaign season was going on in Houston, Texas. One day I was driving and saw that the mayor was having a breakfast dinner at the convention center in my neighborhood. So, I said this is a start to network and get my feet wet and I was determined to meet the mayor as well.

The next week I attended the mayor's breakfast. I did not realize that almost everyone there were influential in the community and were extremely involved in the community. As I sat at my table, I pulled the courage together to talk to the people at my table. I got a lot of information on the candidates running for local offices and got connected to a lady who was a campaign manager for a runner up for Congress. But I told myself before I leave, I will talk to the mayor and get a picture. I accomplished that goal and got to network with many good leaders in the community. This was a start to something new.

Right after the mayor's dinner, I got to work doing my research on the elected officials and the runners for different political offices. The candidate that I picked was a good leader in the community. I got ahold of his campaign manager and got to work. I became his right-hand man. I started to do research and get together different local places that he could speak at. I also would meet with the team once a week. My favorite thing to do was to attend these nice events with different people in the community so he could get the community to get to know who was running for office. The candidate was humble and had a good character. After a couple of months of being involved in his campaign, when it was over, I decided to go back to graduate school.

I went to my mother and sister and told them my plan was to go back to school. They were supper excited and thought that it was the best decision that I had made. I prayed about it and knew that God was speaking. The school that I picked was in Louisiana it was Grambling State University. This was a big step for me. I would be the first out of my mother's kids to get their master's degree. This was also huge because I was overcoming my fear of going back to school. Just because of everything that happened at Oral Roberts University.

Year of Beginnings 2017

So, I went ahead and started my graduate school process. I applied and within a week I got all my stuff in. Then within a couple of weeks I got my acceptance letter. The major I picked was Public Administration. I always had a dream of working in an office for a political office to learn for the elected official. I moved with a relative and walked to campus every day. I was determined to get my degree no matter what.

I really enjoyed my professors. I learned a lot and met a lot of new people. One thing I loved is how motivated these students were about their education. Going to a Historical Black College really showed me so much about how people took pride in their culture.

As I got to know more about the departments, I finally figured out that I wanted to learn about the criminal justice system, so I changed my major to criminal justice. I loved this because my classes were online. This benefited me because I was able to work from home. This was nothing new to me because I was homeschooled. I promised myself in this major I will not make anything less than an A.

Oral Roberts University

VS.

Grambling State University

I had learned a lot from my undergraduate school at Oral Roberts University. This was a Christian private school. The school was different, and the culture was a lot different from a Historic Black College. At ORU there were a lot of rules that we had to follow. I had to go to mandatory chapel twice a week. A dormitory meeting once a week. Curfew was at midnight. The girls and boys could not go to each other's dorms. We did not have any fraternities and sororities because it was a sin. There was not much we could do at this school. There were events but they were kiddy. One thing that I loved was everyone was friendly, and I had a Godly community.

Now at my graduate school Grambling State University, I wanted the full college experience. I knew how to balance my work because of everything I had gone through in undergraduate. The setting at the school was much more comfortable to me. Everyone at the school was nice. One thing I loved about the school was that the students and staff took pride in being African American. There were always activities going on all year around. I really wish ORU would have done more fun things as adults. It helped release a lot of stress from school and made the students take pride in going to a HBCU. There we had concerts, Spring Feast, Homecoming, Bayou Classic and much more. I cannot describe to you the fun and family environments this culture had to offer. I most definitely do not regret going to an HBCU. I feel like this was an opportunity to gain what I missed out on at Oral Roberts University as an undergraduate.

Chapter 12

The Heart of a Grandmother

While in college I finally got my own place. The last year of Graduate school, I got the opportunity to move my grandma in my apartment and help take care of her. This was a huge life changing time. I enjoyed taking care of her. During this time, I had a fulltime job and going to school fulltime. I was honored and grateful that I could do this. I knew God wanted me to do this and take her in.

During this time, I was taught a lot of responsibility. It taught me to be selfless, manage money, and learn to cook. One of my favorite things was to cook for my grandma. Now I was not a big cook before she moved in. But it was through trial-and-error learning to cook. My grandma was so happy with me. I enjoyed running home and catering to her. Her long talks would bring me joy. She spoke so much into my life. Also, during this time I was able to tell my grandma everything that happened to me in my past. I held nothing back and talked to her about things I had never told anyone. I believe God was bringing healing through my testimony. We had moments when I cried and times when I just laughed. But soon things would change.

One day I had come home from work and I had gone into my room. I had heard a loud noise. When I ran out the room my grandmother was laying on the floor. She had fallen and it was a hard fall. I had to call 911 because she was not responding to me. They rushed her to the hospital, and this was a start to something I could not handle by myself.

My grandma's kids had come into town. I had to do the hardest thing and it hurt like hell. But I knew her health was out of my control. I had to tell her kids I could no longer take of her at my house. Later, I found out that she would have to go to a rehabilitation nursing home.

During this time, she started to come around. While this happened, I started to have health problems and had to stop working. But my mother was a great help and stepped in to help me. My grandmother did not want me to get another job. She wanted me to sit with her every day. So, I did not work for about a year. My routine everyday was to do my homework and come sit with my grandma. We would laugh and cry sometimes. But she was a joy that would brighten up any room. People loved her and loved to hear her angelic voice when she would sing.

But as time went on, she was in and out of the hospital and her health started to decline. She started to have a lot of medical problems. It got to the point a lot of times it was hard to see her because it would hurt. We no longer could talk because sometimes she would be out of it. I had to learn how to deal with things on my own. I believe I started to have a peace with God taking her home. I believe the time that my grandma lived with me was God's timing. There was a lot healing that took place. In areas of my life that were broken and I thank God for that. My grandma died June 12, 2019. Her death was hard on me. I had to go to therapy to cope with it and had to surround myself with close friends and loved ones. I still think about her today. But I do not grieve as though I do not have any hope. For I know that she is at peace resting with my heavenly father Jesus Christ. May her legacy live own and every word of wisdom that she gave me show up in my daily life.

Graduation

Five months had gone by since my grandmother's death and I was still going strong in school. In December 2019 it was the big month that I was going to graduate. I was excited because I knew my hard work had paid off. I graduated with a 3.8 GPA and never looked back since. I had overcome a lot of obstacles mentally, spiritually, and emotionally. That day made me proud of myself. It showed me that nothing is impossible.

Words of Encouragement

I would like to tell all my readers this book is not a book to grief with. But to show you major obstacles that I have had to overcome just to get where I am today. It is a dedication to loved ones who have helped me along the way. By reading this book I hope it brought clarity to areas of your life and can say, well, if she went through this, I most defiantly could overcome what I am going through as well. I hope that you no longer live in fear and shame of your past or your present. For God knows what you are experiencing. I hope this is therapeutic for you as well. That the prayers and words that I have given will heal wounds and mend relationships.

www.ingramcontent.com/pod-product-compliance
Lightning Source LLC
Chambersburg PA
CBHW050705160426
43194CB00010B/2005